APR 1 7 2014

APR 1 7 2014

MASERATI

SPEED MACHINES

Julia J. Quinlan

PowerKiDS
press.

New York

Published in 2014 by The Rosen Publishing Group, Inc.
29 East 21st Street, New York, NY 10010

First Edition

Editor: Jennifer Way
Book Design: Greg Tucker
Book Layout: Kate Vlachos

Photo Credits: Cover © iStockphoto.com/Sjoerd van der Wal; pp. 4, 24 (top) Evren Kalinbacak/Shutterstock.com; p. 5 Ferenc Szelepcsenyi/Shutterstock.com; p. 6 ermess/Shutterstock.com; p. 7 AFP/Stringer/Getty Images; pp. 8–9 © Transtock/SuperStock; p. 10 eans/Shutterstock.com; p. 11 Cameron Spencer/Getty Images News/Getty Images; p. 12 © motioncompany/age fotostock; p. 13 Manfred Steinbach/Shutterstock.com; p. 14 Jemny/Shutterstock.com; p. 15 Klemantaski Collection/Hulton Archive/Getty Images; p. 16 Art Konovalov/Shutterstock.com; p. 17 DeepGreen/Shutterstock.com; pp. 18–19, 22 Car Culture/Car Culture Collection/Getty Images; p. 20 Eric Vandeville/Gamma–Rapho/Getty Images; p. 21 Massimiliano Lamagna/Shutterstock.com; p. 23 Vilius Steponenas/Shutterstock.com; p. 24 (bottom) Miguel Medina/AFP/Getty Images; p. 25 Bloomberg/Getty Images; p. 26 Stefan Ataman/Shutterstock.com; p. 27 ChinaFotoPress/Getty Images; pp. 28–29 Philip Lange/Shutterstock.com.

Library of Congress Cataloging-in-Publication Data

Quinlan, Julia J.
    Maserati / by Julia J. Quinlan. — First edition.
        pages cm. — (Speed machines)
    Includes index.
    ISBN 978-1-4777-0808-8 (library binding) — ISBN 978-1-4777-0988-7 (pbk.) —
ISBN 978-1-4777-0989-4 (6-pack)
    1. Maserati automobile—Juvenile literature. I. Title.
    TL215.M34Q56 2014
    629.222—dc23
                                    2013000187

Manufactured in the United States of America

CPSIA Compliance Information: Batch #S13PK8: For Further Information contact Rosen Publishing, New York, New York at 1-800-237-9932

Contents

Racecars to Sports Cars 4

The Maserati Brothers 6

Early Innovators 8

Modern Maseratis 10

Legendary Racecars 12

Championship Racers 14

3500 GT 16

Ghibli 18

Spyder 20

Quattroporte 22

GranTurismo 24

GranCabrio 26

Maserati's Future 28

Comparing Maseratis 30

Glossary 31

Index 32

Websites 32

Racecars to Sports Cars

For nearly a century, Maserati has made eye-catching **luxury** sports cars. This Italian company is known for the speed and power of its stylish cars. Six brothers who loved car racing founded Maserati. The company began by making racecars. When Maserati started to make road cars, it designed them with racecars in mind. Maserati sports cars are fast, with excellent control and handling, just like racecars. Unlike racecars, they are luxurious, comfortable, and practical for everyday driving.

The Maserati Quattroporte is a luxury sports car that Maserati currently makes.

This is the racecar version of the Maserati MC12, which is also produced as a road car.

Maserati has a long and interesting history. The company has been making impressive sports cars for many years and continues to be one of the leading luxury sports car companies today. To remain so successful, Maserati has **innovated**, redesigned, and changed over the years, all while keeping its roots in mind.

The Maserati Brothers

The Maserati brothers founded Maserati in 1914. The brothers' names were Alfieri, Bindo, Carlo, Ettore, Ernesto, and Mario. The six brothers were born in the late 1800s in northern Italy. All of the Maserati brothers, except for Mario, were interested in mechanics and **engineering**. Mario was an artist. Many people think Mario designed the famous trident **logo** that represents the Maserati brand.

The A6GCS was produced between 1953 and 1955. Here, a 1954 model is being driven in a road race for classic sports cars.

The Maserati logo

The other five Maserati brothers worked for many different carmakers and were racecar drivers. In 1914, Alfieri started his own company called Società Anonima Officine Alfieri Maserati. The brothers began car-making by **modifying** existing cars. In 1926, they made the first all-original Maserati model, the Tipo 26.

The Maserati company has changed hands many times since it was founded. In 1937, the Maserati brothers sold their company to the Adolfo Orsi family. Since 1993, Fiat has owned Maserati. Fiat also owns Ferrari and several other car companies.

Early Innovators

Maserati has been innovating since the beginning. The Maserati brothers were passionate about the engineering and mechanics behind creating great cars. They even registered for a patent for one of their **spark plugs** in the 1920s. One of Maserati's most famous innovations was the Maserati Birdcage, created in the early 1960s. The Birdcage was a **chassis** that looked like a series of connected triangles. This chassis design, called the spaceframe, made the Birdcage very sturdy, but very light.

Modern Maseratis are known for their excellent engineering and for their quality and style. They are made to have the speed and control of a racecar. Maserati sports cars are much more comfortable than a racecar, though. The interiors are luxurious and made with high-quality materials, including hand-stitched leather seats.

A special Maserati Birdcage was made in 2005. It honored the Birdcages of the 1960s. It was also made to celebrate the 75th anniversary of the car-design company Pininfarina, which designed this model.

Modern Maseratis

The GranCabrio is Maserati's convertible.

In 2013, Maserati **produced** three models. They are the GranCabrio, the GranTurismo, and the Quattroporte. These three models are meant to represent the three prongs of the Maserati trident. Each model is available in several different versions that vary in price and power. The MC version is the fastest and most powerful. Most of the Maserati models sell for more than $100,000. Although that is a lot of money, they are less expensive in comparison to other luxury sports car brands such as Aston Martin.

Maserati has made very expensive limited-edition models, though. The MC12 started at $1 million! The MC12 was in production from 2004 to 2005 and only 50 models were made. It had 630 horsepower and a V12 engine. The MC12 had a top speed of 205 miles per hour (330 km/h) and could go from 0–62 miles per hour (0–100 km/h) in just 3.8 seconds!

The MC12, shown here, is a supercar. A supercar is a special high-performance sports car. They are usually made in limited numbers and are often very expensive.

Legendary Racecars

The first car the Maserati brothers built together was the Tipo 26. This racecar came out in 1926. It had a 1.5-liter engine and a top speed of 112 miles per hour (180km/h). The Tipo 26 was followed by many more Maserati racecars.

Here is a Maserati in an FIA GT Championship race. This type of racing uses racecar versions of grand tourer, or GT, cars.

The Maserati 4CL is a one-seat racecar made from 1939 through the 1950s. Here, it is being driven in a special race for historic racecars.

In 1967, Maserati took a long break from international racing to focus on its sports cars. In 2004, Maserati came back to racing after 37 years with the MC12 GT1. This car was a combination of a Maserati and a Ferrari. The chassis and gearbox were the same as the Ferrari Enzo. This model had some difficulty being approved for racing competitions because of its power and wide, low design. Once approved, though, this powerful car proved to be a winning racecar. The MC12 GT1 won at the FIA GT Championship in 2005, 2006, and 2007.

Championship Racers

The Maserati Tipo 26 won its class at a race called the Targa Florio and placed ninth overall, in 1926. The car was driven by Alfieri Maserati. The Targa Florio was a sports car racing event held in Sicily, Italy, from 1906 until 1977. Maserati's win at Targa Florio was just the beginning of the long racing tradition of Maserati. Maserati went on to win at the Targa Florio in 1937, 1939, and 1940.

In the Trofeo Maserati, people buy or rent a Trofeo car to use and sign themselves or their team up for races. Then they train and compete.

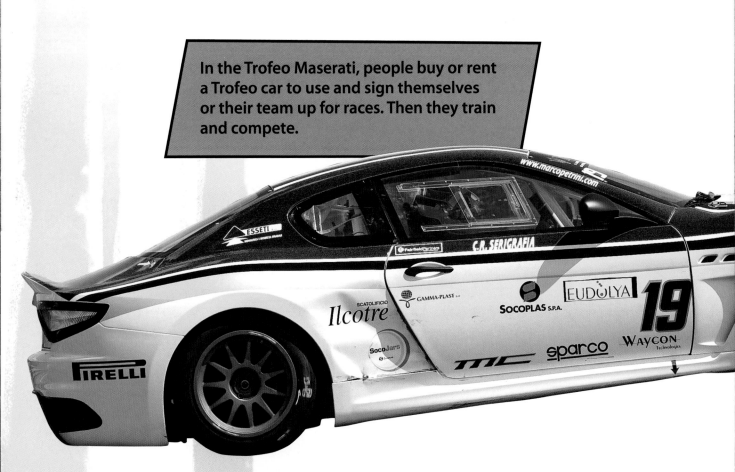

The Targa Florio was an endurance race that was run on Sicily's roads. Here, a car is competing in the 1969 race as it winds through a hilly village's streets.

Today Maserati runs its own racing series for Maserati enthusiasts, called the Trofeo Maserati. These races are held all around the world. Car lovers can sign up to drive a Maserati GranTurismo in a Trofeo race. All of the cars are the same, with the same speed and power, so winning the race is all about the driver's skill.

3500 GT

The 3500 GT was one of the first grand tourers produced by Maserati. Grand tourers are luxury cars that are made for long-distance driving. Maserati wanted the 3500 GT to be powerful and exciting to drive but also have features that made it practical for everyday use. The first 3500 GT came out in 1957 and was produced until 1964. The 3500 GT was Maserati's first really successful road car.

About 2,200 3500 GTs were made and sold during its production years.

3500 GT

Engine size	3.5 liters
Number of cylinders	6
Transmission	Manual
Gearbox	4 speed (5 speeds after 1960)
0–60 mph (0–97 km/h)	8 seconds
Top speed	134 mph (215 km/h)

Before making the 3500 GT, Maserati had focused on making racecars and had trouble getting into the road car mindset.

The 3500 GT was a comfortable grand tourer, but it still had the performance of a racecar. It had a top speed on 134 miles per hour (215 km/h) and a 6-cylinder engine. The 3500 GT was very popular. It was driven by many movie stars of the time.

The convertible version of the 3500 GT was known as the Vignale Spyder. "Vignale" is the name of the company that designed this version, and "spyder" is the name given to the convertible version of many cars.

Ghibli

Maserati introduced the Ghibli in 1967. With a long shark-shaped nose and pop-up headlights, the Ghibli was very eye-catching. It had a top speed on 164.5 miles per hour (265 km/h.) At first, the Ghibli was supposed to have only two seats, but this was changed to a 2+2 design when it went into production. A 2+2 car has two front seats and two small back seats. Most car backseats have space for three passengers. Sports cars that have backseats often have only two seats because this keeps the car's design smaller and sportier. The original Ghibli stopped production in 1973. In 1992, Maserati reintroduced the Ghibli and called it the Ghibli II. The Ghibli II was made from 1992 until 1997. It had a top speed of 153 miles per hour (246 km/h) and a 6-cylinder engine.

Maserati is planning to produce a third version of the Ghibli. It is supposed to come out in 2014.

Here is a 1967 Ghibli, which was part of the first generation of the model.

Ghibli I

Engine size	4.7 liters
Number of cylinders	8
Transmission	Manual
Gearbox	5 speeds
0–60 mph (0–97 km/h)	6.4 seconds
Top speed	164 mph (265 km/h)

Spyder

The Spyder was produced from 2001 until 2007. It was based on the 3200 GT, an earlier Maserati model. It had an all new **transmission** and gearbox, though. It was also lower to the ground. The Spyder was a convertible, but there was also a hardtop version called the Coupé. Both versions had excellent handling and could accelerate, or speed up, very quickly. They could go from 0–60 miles per hour (0–97 km/h) in just 4.9 seconds and had a top speed of 174 miles per hour (280 km/h).

A car with "spider" or "spyder" in its name, like the Maserati Spyder, has a cloth or vinyl roof stretched over a foldable frame. It gets its name because the frame looks a little like a spider's legs.

Spyder

Engine size	4.2 liters
Number of cylinders	8
Transmission	Manual
Gearbox	6 speeds
0–60 mph (0–97 km/h)	4.9 seconds
Top speed	174 mph (280 km/h)

Here is a 2004 Maserati Spyder at a car show.

The Spyder had the excellent engineering and handling for which Maserati is known. Unlike other luxury sports cars, though, it was also practical. Many sports cars, like Ferrari, are so powerful that they are difficult to drive in cities. They are made to be driven on highways, where they can go fast. The Spyder can speed along the highway, but it also handles well in cities.

Quattroporte

The first Quattroporte was introduced in 1963. It was the fastest four-door **sedan** in the world at the time. It had a top speed on 143 miles per hour (230 km/h). That speed was amazing because the Quattroporte was a big car. It was 16 feet (5 m) long and had room for 5 passengers. There were three different generations of the Quattroporte made between 1963 and 1990. A fourth generation was made between 1994 and 2001 and a fifth generation between 2004 and 2012. The sixth generation of Quattroporte began in 2012 and continues to this day.

The 2008 Quattroporte, shown here, was part of the fifth generation of the model.

2012 Quattroporte S

Engine size	4.7 liters
Number of cylinders	8
Transmission	Automatic
Gearbox	6 speeds
0–60 mph (0–97 km/h)	5.3 seconds
Top speed	174 mph (280 km/h)

The fifth generation of Quattroporte was made from 2004 until 2012. The sixth generation went into production in 2012.

Today's Quattroporte is more streamlined than the original. It is also much faster, with a top speed of 174 miles per hour (280 km/h). The Quattroporte's engine was designed by Ferrari. The exterior design of the car was done by Pininfarina. Pininfarina is a design company that has designed many of Ferrari's cars.

GranTurismo

Top: The GranTurismo Sport, shown here, debuted in 2012. It replaced the GranTurismo S. *Bottom*: The GranTurismo MC Stradale is a two-seater, rather than the 2+2 seater that is available in the rest of the GranTurismo line.

The GranTurismo is a two-door coupe that was introduced in 2007. This model has a classic, sleek sports car design courtesy of the Pininfarina design firm. The GranTurismo has a Ferrari-designed engine. Like all Maseratis, the GranTurismo is high-powered, which makes it exciting for drivers who appreciate sports cars with great performance. It comfortably seats four passengers, so it is also practical for everyday use.

The GranTurismo is still in production today. It comes in different versions. There is the GranTurismo S Automatic, the GranTurismo Sport, and the GranTursimo MC. The MC is the newest, most powerful, and most exclusive version. It was designed to make drivers feel like they are driving a racecar while driving a sports car. The MC is the first Maserati to go faster than 186 miles per hour (300 km/h).

The GranCabrio is based on the GranTurismo. In fact, in the United States, this model is often called the GranTurismo Convertible.

GranTurismo MC

Engine size	4.7 liters
Number of cylinders	8
Transmission	Automatic
Gearbox	6 speeds
0–60 mph (0–97 km/h)	4.8 seconds
Top speed	186 mph (300 km/h)

GranCabrio

The GranCabrio is the convertible version of the GranTurismo. It is Maserati's first four-seat convertible. It has a soft top instead of a hard top. Hard tops are more popular in luxury sports cars, but this makes the car heavier. A heavy car has a harder time accelerating and going fast. By choosing a soft top, the GranCabrio can have the same power and speed as the GranTurismo.

The GranCabrio MC was introduced at the 2012 Paris Motor Show.

Première Mondiale

GranCabrio MC

Engine size	4.7 liters
Number of cylinders	8
Transmission	Automatic
Gearbox	6 speeds
0–60 mph (0–97 km/h)	4.9 seconds
Top speed	180 mph (289 km/h)

Convertibles like the GranCabrio often have roofs made of a tough fabric called canvas.

The GranCabrio first came out in 2010 and is still in production today. There are three different GranCabrio models. They are the GranCabrio, the GranCabrio Sport, and the GranCabrio MC. The MC is the latest GranCabrio model. It is similar to the other GranCabrio models, but with a few changes to its design. The front of the car was lengthened by 2 inches (5 cm). The back of the car was also changed to make the car more **aerodynamic**.

Maserati's Future

Every year, Maserati comes out with new and exciting models. Although the company is best known for its fast sports cars, Maserati will be producing an SUV in 2014. The Kubang is a four-door SUV with a V8 engine. It will be manufactured in America, unlike all other Maseratis, which are made in Italy. It shares a platform, or basic structure, with the Jeep Grand Cherokee. Jeep is part of Chrysler, which is owned by Fiat. Fiat is Maserati's parent company.

Maserati has been in business for nearly 100 years. It has a reputation as the maker of some of the most desirable sports cars in the world. That is because as Maserati innovates and changes with the times, the company never loses sight of its racing roots and its commitment to quality.

Here is a Maserati Kubang on display at a 2011 car show.

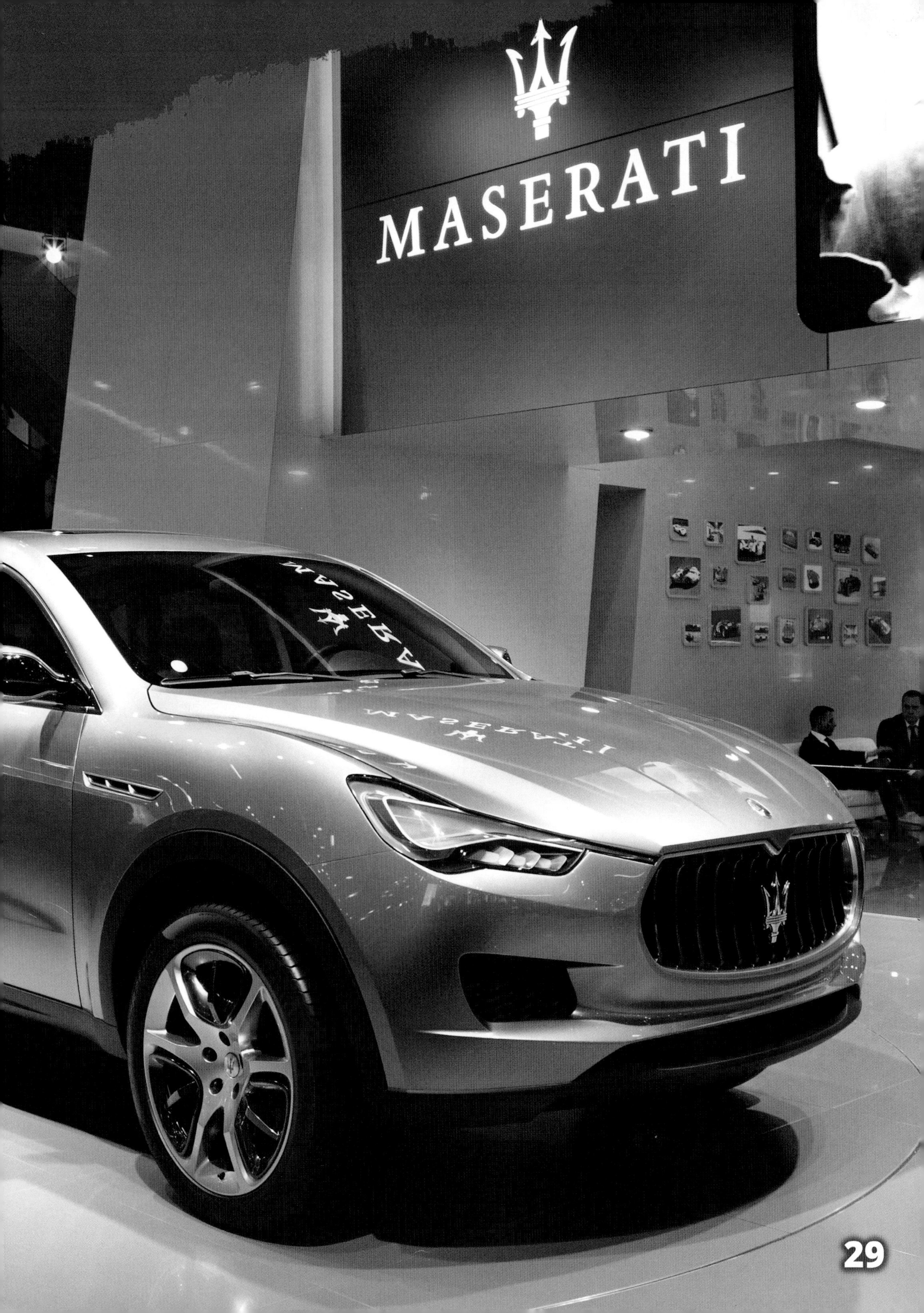
MASERATI

Comparing Maseratis

CAR	YEARS MADE	TRANSMISSION	TOP SPEED	FACT
3500 GT	1957–1964	4–speed manual (1957–1960) 5–speed manual (1960–1964)	134 mph (215 km/h)	The 3500 GT was Maserati's first large-volume production.
Ghibli	1967–1973, 1992–1997	5–speed manual	164 mph (265 km/h)	This car is named for a desert storm wind.
Spyder	2001–2007	6–speed manual	174 mph (280 km/h)	The Spyder is also called the 4200 GT.
Quattroporte	2004–	6–speed manual	174 mph (280 km/h)	*Quattroporte* means "four doors" in Italian.
GranTurismo	2007–	6–speed automatic	186 mph (300 km/h)	*Gran turismo* means "gran tourer" in Italian.
GranCabrio	2010–	6–speed automatic	180 mph (289 km/h)	Designed by the car-design firm Pininfarina.

Glossary

aerodynamic (er-oh-dy-NA-mik) Made to move through the air easily.

chassis (CHA-see) The part that holds up the body of a car.

engineering (en-juh-NEER-ing) The planning and building of engines, machines, roads, and bridges.

innovated (ih-nuh-VAYT-ed) Created something new.

logo (LOH-goh) A picture or phrase that stands for a team or company.

luxury (LUK-shuh-ree) Comforts and beauties of life that are not necessary.

modifying (MAH-dih-fy-ing) Changing something.

produced (pruh-DOOSD) Made something.

sedan (sih-DAN) A car that seats four or more people.

spark plugs (SPAHRK PLUGZ) The devices in a car's engine that ignite the fuel mixture using an electric spark.

transmission (trans-MIH-shun) A group of car parts that includes the gears for changing speeds and that conveys the power from the engine to the machine's rear wheels.

Index

A
aerodynamic, 27
Aston Martin, 10

B
brothers, 4, 6–8, 12

C
chassis, 8, 13
Chrysler, 28
company, 4–5, 7, 23, 28
competitions, 13
convertible, 20, 26
coupe, 24

D
door(s), 22, 24, 28, 30
driver(s), 7, 15, 24–25

E
engine, 11–12, 17–18,
    23–24, 28

F
Ferrari, 7, 13, 21,
    23–24
Fiat, 7, 28

G
gearbox, 13, 20
generation(s), 22
grand tourer(s), 16–17

H
handling, 4, 20, 21
headlights, 18
highway, 21
horsepower, 11

I
interiors, 8
Italy, 6, 14, 28

J
Jeep, 28

M
materials, 8
mechanics, 6, 8
model(s), 7, 10–11, 13, 20,
    24, 27–28

P
passengers, 18, 22, 24
Pininfarina, 23–24, 30
production, 11, 18, 25,
    27, 30

R
racecar(s), 4, 7–8, 12–13,
    17, 25

S
seat(s), 8, 18, 24, 26

T
transmission, 20
trident, 6, 10

Websites

Due to the changing nature of Internet links, PowerKids Press has developed an online list of websites related to the subject of this book. This site is updated regularly. Please use this link to access the list: www.powerkidslinks.com/smach/maser/